This book is dedicated to children everywhere, for they will inherit the Earth and then strive to right the wrongs of previous generations; both for their own survival, and because it's the right thing to do.

And, for Becky.

Ellia and Alex
from
Grandma Sintek

www.mascotbooks.com

What's Going Down in Prairie Dog Town?

For more information, please contact:
Mascot Books
620 Herndon Parkway #320
Herndon, VA 20170
info@mascotbooks.com

Library of Congress Control Number: 2018905398

CPSIA Code: PRT0718A
ISBN-13: 978-1-68401-772-0

Printed in the United States

What's Going Down in Prairie Dog Town?

Alan J. Bartels

illustrated by Hannah Segura

Foreword

I fell in love with prairie dogs from the very first moment I saw them. A friend drove me to a prairie dog town and we watched the rabbit-sized little animals through our binoculars. A male was standing upright on the mound of earth that surrounded a burrow. He could see a bit further from up there and was watching out for enemies. Nearby, a female was stretched out, snoozing. When another female came over they stood upright, embraced, and gave each other a prairie dog kiss.

There were other family groups nearby. Everywhere young ones were playing, leaping at each other, and rolling on the ground, wrestling. Then a bird of prey appeared overhead and at once the male made loud, chirping alarm calls. Other males did the same, and all the prairie dogs disappeared below the ground.

I knew that their burrows formed a great network of passages underground with separate rooms dug out for nurseries, sleeping, toilets, and so on. And, as you will read in this book, these burrows provide safe places for so many different animals. I would have given anything to be able to follow the prairie dogs that day and explore their wonderful underground home.

Even more, I wished I could turn the clock back 100 years and find myself on the prairies as they were before widespread settlement, stretching as far as the eye could see, and for hundreds of miles beyond that. Alas, those days have gone, along with the great bison herds that roamed there.

Agriculture has taken over most of the prairies. Communities have sprung up and destroyed even more land. Most of the prairie dog towns have gone too. How sad it is that even those few which remain are often destroyed to reduce competition for grass between prairie dogs and cattle, or as a precaution for horses and cows that might stumble into a prairie dog burrow and break a leg. (Though I have never actually heard of this happening.)

Prairie dogs were here long before us—part of a wonderful prairie world. Don't you think we should try really hard to protect these adorable little creatures? Thank goodness there are people working to conserve and restore the prairies to make sure there are places for the prairie dogs and the many other creatures who depend on them for shelter and food.

I am so glad my friend Alan decided to write this book. He cares passionately about saving the prairie world. At the end of this book, we've provided information so you can learn how you can get involved in Jane Goodall's Roots & Shoots program and learn what you can do to help Alan and all of us who are working to make this a better world for animals and people.

— Jane Goodall

One day on his way home from school, Tyler saw a
strange creature on the sidewalk. It wasn't a cat,
or a dog, or a rabbit, or a tree squirrel. *What is this
thing?* he wondered.

The animal looked scared and alone, so Tyler decided
to take it home and try to help it.

Back home, Tyler opened the encyclopedia that his grandfather gave him and searched the pages until he found what he was looking for—the animal was a prairie dog! Reading that prairie dogs live in large family groups made Tyler sad to see this one all alone.

Tyler named his new friend "Penny" for her coppery color, and fixed up a cardboard box with water, food, and a small towel for Penny to use as a blanket.

Penny, who had been away from home for what seemed like a long time, was very hungry. She eagerly ate the green grass that Tyler picked for her.

That night, Tyler had a bad dream about the time he got lost in a large store. He was afraid he'd never see his mommy again. When he woke up, he couldn't help but wonder if Penny missed her mommy.

The next day, Tyler told his father that he wanted to take Penny back to her home because that is where she belongs—with her family. Tyler's father was very proud of his son, and they took Penny to the prairie dog town in the hills behind their house.

When Penny arrived, her father was upset that she had been gone for so long, but was happy she was home again, safe and sound. Her family feared that a coyote or a hawk had caught her!

It was a wonderful time of year in Prairie Dog Town. Wildflowers were blooming and meadowlarks and other birds were singing. There were lots of other interesting neighbors, too.

Penny and her family munched down the green grass all day long, keeping it short so they could watch for coyotes and other animals that liked to eat prairie dogs.

Everyone was barking about the arrival of burrowing owls. Every year they came to Prairie Dog Town to hatch their eggs. They borrowed burrows from the prairie dogs like so many other animals do.

Penny thought the owls peeking up out of the holes in the ground looked funny. She wondered where the burrowing owls would live if there was no place for them to stay in Prairie Dog Town.

There were babies at the swift fox den too—
three of them! They wrestled around in one big
furry ball and barked playfully at one another.

Sometimes the mother fox would hunt her
prairie dog neighbors. Penny didn't think that
was very neighborly, considering the foxes lived
in a burrow her family had dug.

Penny's grandfather once told her that when he was young, there were many more swift foxes and many more prairie dogs. Penny wondered why there weren't as many foxes or prairie dogs these days, and wondered where the swift foxes would live if there were no burrows for them in Prairie Dog Town.

While the prairie dogs ate grass, rested, and watched for predators, neighbors were always coming and going.

Black and yellow tiger salamanders lived in the underground burrows, sometimes even sharing Penny's room with her. Box turtles, rattlesnakes, beetles, and bullsnakes lived there, too.

After a day of playing and eating grass and purple flowers, Penny's mother gathered the family in their underground home.

Great horned owls and coyotes were especially brave in the darkness and always eager for a prairie dog dinner.

With her many brothers and sisters cuddled beside her, Penny slept through the night, happy that Tyler had brought her home.

Prairie chickens woke Penny up the next morning. Their puffy air sacs, strange booming noises, and fancy dancing caused the prairie dogs to stop and watch the performance.

Penny enjoyed these shows and wondered where the prairie chickens would dance if there was no Prairie Dog Town.

Back at school, Tyler was reading about prairie dogs in the library. He learned that prairie dog towns like Penny's once covered millions of acres in North America, but are much rarer today.

He also learned about the black-footed ferret, a sleek, weasel-like animal that hunts prairie dogs for food, and like many other animals, uses their burrows as a place to live and raise their young.

Tyler learned that black-footed ferrets are now very rare, and that made him sad. He had a nice place to live with a lot of land for his brothers and sisters to explore, but he got very sad at the thought of prairie dog towns being destroyed, leaving many animals with no place to live.

That night, Tyler overheard his parents talking about a man who wanted to buy some of their land to build houses on.

His dad said the man offered a lot of money that they could use to pay off the house and cars, and even buy new bicycles and video games for Tyler and his siblings.

The thought of a brand new bike made Tyler smile. But then he thought of Penny and her family, and all the other animals that lived in the hills behind their home. What would his parents do?

The next day, Penny was eating an especially tasty flower when her mom barked for everyone to hide in the burrow. *Was it a hawk, or a dog, or a coyote?* Penny wondered as she ran.

After a few minutes, Penny peeked out of the burrow. She saw a person wandering around Prairie Dog Town with funny-looking gadgets.

She didn't know it, but it was the man hoping to buy the land where Prairie Dog Town sat. Tyler saw him, too, and knew he had to talk to his father.

Tyler looked around at all of the neighborhoods with new houses and remembered how scared Penny looked when he discovered her.

"Dad, what will happen to the prairie dogs if houses are built on the land?" Tyler asked, holding back tears.

"Well son," Tyler's father said. "I guess they would have to find another place to live."

Tyler couldn't imagine the prairie dogs and other animals being able to find another place to live, and he started to cry.

"You know," Tyler's father said, "I bought this land when you were born because it was where I played when I was your age. There were many more prairie dogs like Penny around here back then, and lots of other animals too. It seemed like there was enough space for all of the living things."

Tyler knew things had changed since then, and he wasn't so sure it was for the better.

"Son," his father began again. "Your mother and I decided not to sell the land after all. This is a special place to me, and I know now it is a special place to you, too."

And over in Prairie Dog Town, just as Tyler's father asked the contractor to leave, Penny hugged her father, too.

Tyler was happy. For now, Prairie Dog Town was safe. There was still a place for Penny, her family, and all of their neighbors to live.

And as Tyler looked around Prairie Dog Town, he knew he would always do everything he could to make sure there always would be.

Historic Distribution of Prairie Dogs

White-tailed prairie dog

Black-tailed prairie dog

Utah prairie dog

Gunnison's prairie dog

Mexican prairie dog

Current ranges of the five prairie dog subspecies are unknown. All have been significantly reduced from historic levels, and continue to dwindle due to lack of local, state, and federal protection.

Many of the animals in this story can be seen in real life on or near Switzer Ranch in Nebraska. calamusoutfitters.com.

Visit these websites to learn more about prairie dogs, the threats they face, and conservation efforts to save them.

- Prairie Dog Pals: prairiedogpals.org

- Prairie Dog Coalition: humanesociety.org/about/departments/prairie_dog_coalition

- National Black-footed Ferret Conservation Center: blackfootedferret.org

A Note from the Author

This book began during breakfast with friends Susan Elmore, John Murphy, Sarah Sortum, Debra Hann, Tom Mangelsen, and Jane Goodall after watching greater prairie chickens on Bruce and Sue Ann Switzer's ranch.

"You should write a children's book about the plight of prairie dogs called *What's Going Down in Prairie Dog Town?*" Susan told me.

I knew this was an important issue to bring to light. After sharing a Nebraska Sandhills sunrise with Jane Goodall, my conservation inspiration since childhood, I was determined.

I know that many other species suffer when prairie dog towns are destroyed. One species, the black-footed ferret, hasn't lived wild in my home state of Nebraska during my lifetime.

According to some estimates, development of land for agriculture, roads, homes, cities, and industry has reduced the range of prairie dogs to just one percent of the 700 million acres the species originally occupied. And yet the destruction continues.

While working on this book one day, I visited a small prairie dog town where I used to watch burrowing owls, prairie chickens, meadowlarks, badgers, and of course, prairie dogs.

When I got there that day, the grass was longer than usual, and I instantly knew something was wrong. The prairie dogs—were gone!

The fact that the landowner poisoned the small, five-acre prairie dog town within his 2,000-acre property made me feel sick, but it strengthened my resolve.

It was up to me to tell their story.

Photo credit: Thomas D. Mangelsen

Author Alan J. Bartels and his conservationist mentor Jane Goodall

Jane Goodall's Roots & Shoots Program

Jane Goodall was a young woman of only 26 years when she left her native England in 1960 to work in Africa. Her groundbreaking work with wild chimpanzees and role as a United Nations Messenger of Peace has inspired generations of youth around the world.

Jane Goodall's Roots & Shoots organization was born in Tanzania, Africa, after Dr. Goodall met in 1991 with a dozen local teenagers searching for solutions to complex problems in their community. The youth service organization now has chapters in more than 100 countries around the world where youth have the ability to make positive change each and every day.

Jane Goodall believes every one of us can help make our world a better place for both people and animals. Visit **rootsandshoots.org** for more information or to learn how to start your own Roots & Shoots chapter.

The author and illustrator are donating proceeds from the sale of this book to Jane Goodall's Roots & Shoots program.

Photo credit: Alan J. Bartels

Black-tailed prairie dogs at Fort Niobrara National Wildlife Refuge in Nebraska.